LUST

AT FIRST SWIPE

*"I am so impressed by your aphorisms...
they densely compact a delicious kernel
of truth in an elegant shell of wit."*

Stephen Fry

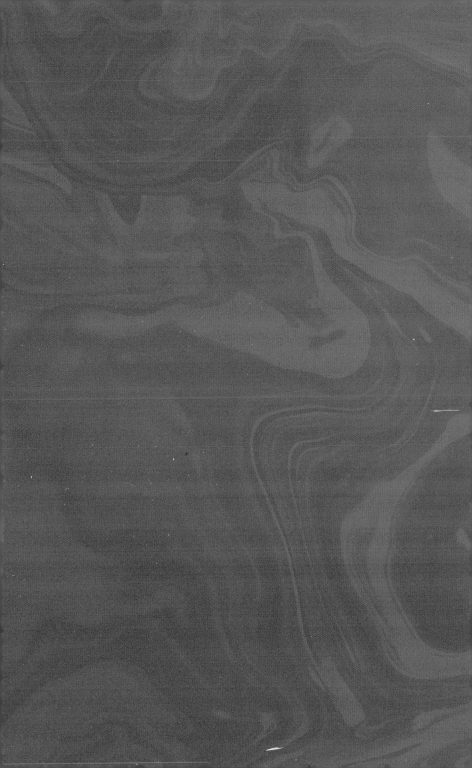

A Note on the QRs

Scattered throughout this book you'll notice
QR (Quick Response) codes. Just scan them
with your phone and enjoy Robert's written
and video commentaries on his work.
Have fun!

ALSO BY ROBERT EDDISON

PUBLISHED:

Peeing is Relieving (Unicorn Publishing Group, 2021)

Wisdom & Wordplay (Filament Publishing, 2017)

No Offence (CHE Publications, 1975)

CONTRIBUTED TO:

Resilient Voices Series (Book Brilliance Publishing, 2021)

Taking Control of OCD (Constable & Robinson, 2011)

Talent for Tomorrow (Bow Publications Ltd., 1963)

STAGE PLAYS:

Commanding Voices (New End Theatre, Hampstead, 2002)

The Lame Duck (The Little Theatre, St Martin's Lane, 1971)

Conscience Factor (The Little Theatre, St Martin's Lane, 1969)

White Suicide (The Little Theatre, St Martin's Lane, 1967)

The Interior Decorators (Southwark Theatre, c.1965)

IN PREPARATION:

MIND S-T-R-E-T-C-H-E-R-S (Eddison Wordplay Ltd., 2022)

INTRODUCTION

As a lifelong Wildean, I consider Oscar Wilde to be a
central exponent of pithy one-liners, along with the likes of
La Rochefoucauld and Mark Twain. Indeed, apart from being a
renowned playwright, Wilde was also a master
aphorist. "I am not young enough to know everything" takes some
beating. In being witty, provocative and deliciously
subversive, this has all the hallmarks of a top-notch maxim.

What about: "Nothing kills lust quicker than cohabitation" or "Fall
in love at first sight and you risk falling out at second"? Although
not by Wilde, I hope they could stand up next to his – and I'd even
like to think that Oscar himself would have agreed. After all, despite
being a literary giant, he was deeply humble and self-critical under a
surface arrogance and was quick to acknowledge talent in others.

But to truly please Wilde, and to count myself among the ranks of
the world's great aphorists, I must offer up two things -
quality and quantity. With 40,000 original maxims on a wide
variety of subjects already in the bag, I think I can tick quantity off
the list. As for the quality, I will let you, the reader, be the judge. In
Wilde's own words: "If one cannot enjoy reading a book over and
over again, there is no use in reading it at all." I hope that in Lust
at First Swipe you have found that book and will be reading it time
and time again. Enjoy!

Robert Eddison

IT'S OUR HEADS WE LOSE WHEN HEAD OVER HEELS IN LOVE

BEAUTY,
LIKE LOVE,
BRINGS OUT
THE BEST IN US

———————

EVEN THE
LOVE OF OUR LIFE
STARTED AS A STRANGER

FALL IN LOVE
AT FIRST SIGHT
AND YOU RISK
FALLING OUT
AT SECOND

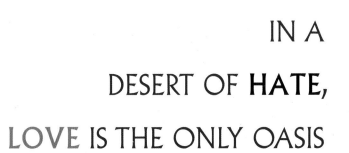

IN A

DESERT OF **HATE,**

LOVE IS THE ONLY OASIS

IF WE EAT
WHAT WE FANCY
WITH OUR TEETH,
WE EAT
WHOM WE FANCY
WITH OUR EYES

NOTHING
KILLS LUST
QUICKER THAN
COHABITATION

....

SEX IS ONLY DIRTY IF YOU HAVEN'T WASHED

LOVE ECLIPSES HATE
AS LIGHT THE DARK

Look Closer!

THE MOON WAS NEVER DESIGNED TO PUT STARS INTO LOVERS' EYES

......

LOVE IS A

CONSTANT,

WHOSE FOCUS

IS THE ONLY

VARIABLE

MOST
LOVE RATS
COME HANDSOME

· · · · · · · · · · · · · · · ·

PORNOGRAPHY IS

IN THE *GROIN* OF

THE BEHOLDER

THOSE WHO
CAN SAY
'THANK YOU',
'SORRY'
AND
'I LOVE YOU'
HAVE THE WORLD
AT THEIR FEET

SEX,

LIKE BREAKFAST,

IS A MEAL BEST

TAKEN IN BED

———

LUST IS TO PASSION

WHAT A SPARK IS

TO TINDER

————————

MOST ONE-NIGHT STANDS ARE SPENT LYING DOWN

PURE LUST CAN BE DELICIOUSLY IMPURE

Look Closer!

LUSTFUL LOVERS WHO SLEEP TOGETHER RARELY DO

Look Closer!

EVEN TEETOTALLERS CAN BE DRUNK ON LUST

A HEART **ON FIRE**

SPARKS THE LOVER'S

SMOULDERING KISS

THE HEART'S
BLIND SIDE
OFTEN SEES CLEAREST

LOVE IS TO ORBIT
AROUND THE SUN OF
YOUR LIFE

THE APPLE OF
SOMEONE'S EYE
RISKS BEING
DEVOURED

EVEN THE SANE
CAN FALL MADLY
IN LOVE

ONLY A PRIVILEGED FEW
ARE LOVED FOR WHO
THEY **REALLY** ARE

TO COURT THE PERFECT PARTNER IS TO COURT DISAPPOINTMENT

Look Closer!

YOUNGSTERS WHO FALL IN LOVE CAN FORGET TO OPEN THE PARACHUTE

Look Closer!

LOVE OFTEN BECKONS TO THOSE IN LUST

NOT ALL
LOVE IS
LAUNCHED
ON THE
ROCKET
OF LUST

OH TO BE SWEPT OFF OUR FEET BY THE RISING TIDE OF LUST!

LOVE CAN'T BE FULLY
MEASURED UNTIL LOST

Look Closer!

◇◇◇◇◇◇◇◇◇◇◇◇◇◇◇◇◇◇◇◇◇◇◇◇◇◇◇◇◇◇◇◇◇◇

LOVE IS WHAT REMAINS
AFTER LUST'S TIDE
HAS EBBED

◇◇◇◇◇◇◇◇◇◇◇◇◇◇◇◇◇◇◇◇◇◇◇◇◇◇◇◇◇◇◇◇◇◇

DROWN YOUR ENEMIES IN
LOVE AND THEY WILL NEVER
FORGIVE YOU

VERTIGO DOESN'T
STOP US FROM
FALLING IN LOVE

ROMANTIC LOVE
COMES IN
EVERY COLOUR
UNDER THE MOON

LOVE ENABLES US TO
BE FULLY OURSELVES

GIVING TOUGH LOVE
CAN *ITSELF* BE TOUGH

STEAMY
PASSION
IS *LUST*
ON THE *BOIL*

IF LOVE ONLY LASTS AS
LONG AS YOUR WIFE'S
GOOD LOOKS,
IT'S NOT LOVE

LOVE TRANSFORMS
LUST'S BASE METAL
INTO GOLD

THE BEST
PRESENTS
COME FROM
THE
UNWRAPPED
HEART

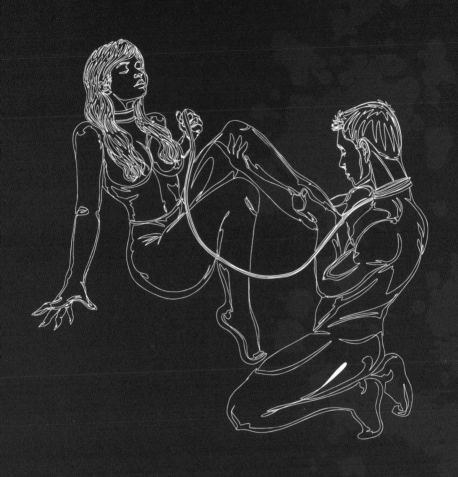

BLASPHEMY IS TO WORSHIP
ANOTHER HUMAN BEING

TO THE SADIST, INFLICTING
PAIN IS A LABOUR OF LOVE

SEX CAN EITHER DISSOLVE
OR CEMENT FRIENDSHIP

Look Closer!

NOTHING KILLS FLIRTATION
QUICKER THAN CONQUEST

NAKED LUST
TOO OFTEN
COMES
DRESSED AS
LOVE

THOSE
GOVERNED
BY THE **HEART**
SHOULD FORM
A COALITION
WITH THE **HEAD**

STARRY-EYED
LOVERS
SHINE
BRIGHTEST
AT NIGHT

THERE IS

NO

MEDICATION

FOR

LOVE'S FEVER

SEX IS WASTED ON THE MONOGAMOUS

YOU CAN ONLY MAKE LOVE TO THE SAME VIRGIN ONCE

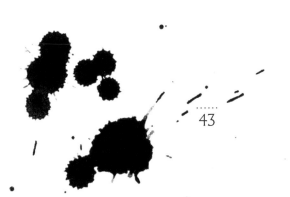

FRIENDSHIP'S
SHOCK ABSORBER
EVENS OUT
LIFE'S BUMPS

. . . .

IF LOVE FLOATS
ON EMOTION,
REASON DROWNS
IN IT

IF ROMANCE IS DEAD,
THERE IS ALWAYS
NECROPHILIA

LUST IS TO
LOVE WHAT THE
GOURMAND IS TO
THE *GOURMET*

IF LOVE STIRS THE HEART,

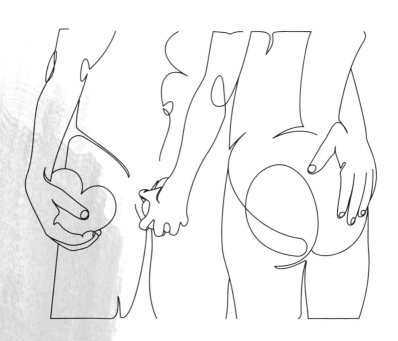

LUST STIRS THE GROIN

TO STATE THAT
SEX IS ONLY
FOR PROCREATION
IS LIKE SAYING
THE SEA ONLY
EXISTS TO
SUPPORT FISH

THE LOVE WE
DENY TO OTHERS
WE ALSO DENY TO
OURSELVES

WE FALL IN LOVE
QUICKER THAN WE
FALL OUT OF IT

. . .

IF LUST PUTS BODY
BEFORE HEART,
LOVE DOES THE
REVERSE

LOVE BLAZES

MOST

FIERCELY

ON THE

SMOKING

COALS

OF LUST

WHIRLWIND ROMANCES CAN
PRESAGE A MARITAL TSUNAMI

◇◇◇◇

IT'S AS WELL TO GET ON
WITH THE PERSON YOU WANT
TO GET OFF WITH

◇◇◇◇

THERE IS AS MUCH CHEMISTRY
BETWEEN HATERS AS
BETWEEN LOVERS

WOULD THAT LUST ALWAYS

BRIDGED US TO THE FAR

BANK OF LOVE

. . . . . .

OUR FEARS

ARE BEST SMOTHERED

IN *LOVE'S PILLOW*

LOVE MAKES LIFE WORTH DYING FOR

STRONG SEXUAL
ATTRACTION
CAN DRIVE ONE TO
DISTRACTION

. . . .

SWEET-TALKING
LOVERS HAVE NO
STOMACH FOR
SOUR GRAPES

. . . .

THERE IS
NOTHING LIKE
SEX TOURISM
TO BROADEN
THE LIBIDO

THERE ARE TWO SIDES
TO EVERY LOVE TRIANGLE

CONDITIONAL LOVE IS A CONTRADICTION IN TERMS

THE
DIFFERENCE
BETWEEN
LUST
AND
LOVE
IS
SKIN
DEEP

ONLY UNCONDITIONAL LOVE

WORKS MIRACLES

Look Closer!

COMPASSION IS THE

INCOME FROM

LOVE'S CAPITAL

Look Closer!

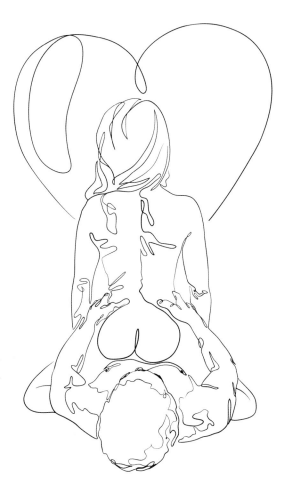

MORE PEOPLE FALL IN
LUST WITHOUT LOVE
THAN IN LOVE WITHOUT LUST

VIRGINITY
IS ONE
OF THE
FEW THINGS
WE ENJOY
LOSING

HER ARDENT
ADMIRERS
PUT THE
ENGLISH ROSE
IN CLOVER

LOVE IS
THE ROOT
OF ALL VIRTUE

• • • • • • • • • • • • • •

REAL LOVE IS ONLY
POSSIBLE WHEN IT IS
NOT A SUBSTITUTE
FOR SELF-ESTEEM

DESPITE BEING MADE FOR EACH OTHER, COUPLES DON'T ALWAYS MAKE IT

THE HERNIA OF HATE IS QUICKLY STRANGULATED BY LOVE

IF LOVE
DID NOT
RIDE ON
LUST,
THE OLD
WOULD FALL
IN LOVE AS
READILY AS
THE YOUNG

CUPID,
UNLIKE LIGHTNING,
OFTEN
STRIKES
TWICE

LOVE ON THE REBOUND
RISKS BOUNCING LIKE
A BAD CHEQUE

LOTHARIOS ARE
ON CONSTANT
LOOKOUT FOR
THE LUST OF
THEIR LIFE

SEX IS TO GO ALL
THE WAY WITHOUT
LEAVING YOUR BED

NOTHING KILLS
EROTICISM QUICKER
THAN NUDITY

LOVE A NARCISSIST AND YOU'LL HAVE A LIFELONG RIVAL FOR YOUR AFFECTIONS

NEVER BELIEVE THE MAN
WHO ONLY TELLS YOU
ONCE THAT HE LOVES YOU

SOME FALL IN **LOVE** AS
EASILY AS THEY FALL
INTO **BED**

LUST AND LOVE **ARE**
CLEAVAGES APART

LOVE
WITHOUT
LUST
IS LIKE
STRAWBERRIES
WITHOUT CREAM

LOVE IS A GUEST THAT
RARELY OVERSTAYS
ITS WELCOME

LOVE, LIKE GOD,
CANNOT BE COMMANDED,
ONLY OBEYED

THE WAY **NOT** TO
FIND LOVE
IS TO SEARCH FOR IT

LOVE
COMES FROM
THE HEART;
COMPASSION
FROM THE GUT;
ANGER FROM
THE SPLEEN

NOTHING BLINDS OUR JUDGEMENT
QUICKER THAN LUST

NYMPHOMANIACS
ARE BEST
COUPLED WITH
INSOMNIACS

LUST
IS TO EAT YOUR PARTNER FOR BREAKFAST;
LOVE
IS TO COOK IT FOR HIM

LOVE IS TO HATE
WHAT CREATIVITY IS
TO DESTRUCTION

◇◇◇◇◇

IF FALLING OUT
OF LUST IS INEVITABLE,
FALLING OUT OF LOVE IS NOT

◇◇◇◇◇

INTIMACY ALLOWS FOR THE
DISCARDING OF BOUNDARIES

LOVE
SOMEONE
TOO
MUCH
AND
YOU
COULD
SMOTHER
THEIR
ABILITY
TO
RECIPROCATE

MANY

A

LOVE

TRIANGLE

FAILS

TO

SQUARE

ITS

DIFFERENCES

WITH

CIRCULAR

ARGUMENT

IF GRAVITATIONAL
ATTRACTION PULLS YOU **DOWN**,
SEXUAL ATTRACTION PULLS YOU **UP**

◇◇◇◇◇

IF BEING LOVED IS THE ULTIMATE
COMPLIMENT, BEING IMITATED IS THE
PENULTIMATE ONE

◇◇◇◇◇

IF BEAUTY IS IN THE EYE OF THE
BEHOLDER, IT IS IN *BOTH* EYES
OF THE BESOTTED

UNCONDITIONAL LOVE COMES WITH ALL HEARTSTRINGS ATTACHED

LOVE'S FIERCE SUN IS TOO OFTEN
CLOUDED BY SELF-DOUBT

NOTHING CONCENTRATES
THE HEART LIKE LOVE

LOVE IS NEVER AN ACT OF WILL

LOVE REKINDLES LUST'S
DYING EMBERS

WOULD THAT
THE BLIND COULD
FALL IN LOVE AT FIRST SIGHT

IF LUST RIDES
ON ATTRACTION,
LOVE RIDES ON EMPATHY

LOOK FOR LOVE AND YOU'LL PREVENT IT CATCHING YOU UNAWARES

FORBIDDEN LOVE
HAS TO BE
THE *SWEETEST*

IF PARTNERS AGREE ON EVERYTHING,
THERE IS SOMETHING WRONG

●　●　●

HELL **ON STILTS IS FOR A WARRING**
COUPLE TO MEET UP THERE

●　●　●

IF TRUE LOVE ISN'T A JOINT BANK
ACCOUNT, WHAT IS?

TO FALL IN LOVE WITH NARCISSUS IS TO BE PIPPED TO THE POST

LOVE IS WHEN
TROUBLE
IS *NO TROUBLE*

FOR LOVERS, THE
AGEING NIGHT
IS ALWAYS YOUNG

LUST AND LOVE ENJOY SINGING FROM THE **SAME** HYMN SHEET

Look Closer!

WOULD THAT WE STOPPED MISTAKING THE CENTRE OF **OUR** UNIVERSE FOR THE CENTRE OF *THE* UNIVERSE

Look Closer!

MARRIAGE IS WHEN
THE MAKE-UP
COMES
OFF

LUST
IS NOT LOVE

– BUT IT JOLLY WELL HELPS

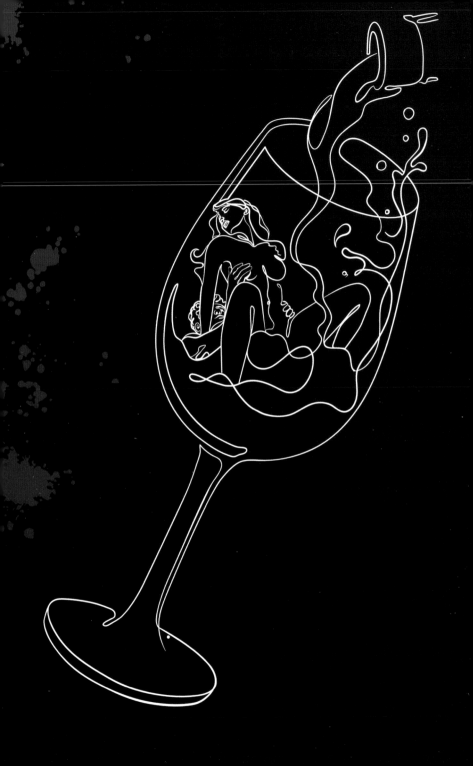

FOOD IS AS MUCH ENRICHED BY WINE AS LOVE IS BY SEX

RELATIONSHIPS

ARE BEST AVOIDED

BY EMBARKING ON

A LIFELONG SEARCH

FOR THE IDEAL

PARTNER

Look Closer!

BEING SINGLE IS PREFERABLE
TO BEING LINKED TO AN
INSIGNIFICANT OTHER

WITHOUT DEEP ROOTS,
LOVE'S OAK TREE GETS
BLOWN AWAY

IT'S HARD FOR THOSE WHO
CAN'T LOVE THEMSELVES
TO LOVE OTHERS

APPS
HELP US
TO FIND
LUST AT FIRST *SWIPE*

PLAY

HARD TO GET

AND

YOU MIGHT

NOT BE GOT

IF THE **LOVER** FLIES THROUGH LIFE, THE **HATER** TRIPS OVER IT

MUTUAL LOVE COMES HARD TO THE EMOTIONALLY NEEDY

WIThOUT LUST, LOVE LACKS ITS EDGE

◊

LOVE
IS AN
INTOXICATING
MIX OF
EMPATHY
AND LUST

THOSE WHO LOVE EACH OTHER TO BITS MAY HAVE TO PICK THEM UP LATER

Look Closer!

HATE-FUELLED ENMITY
IS DISEMPOWERED
BY LOVE

Look Closer!

LOVE DEPRIVATION
OFTEN FAST-TRACKS
US TO MATERIALISM

GOD HAS NO MONOPOLY OF UNCONDITIONAL LOVE

INFATUATION'S

SALT WATER

IS BETTER THAN

NOTHING

SEX
IS INTIMACY
ON
STILTS

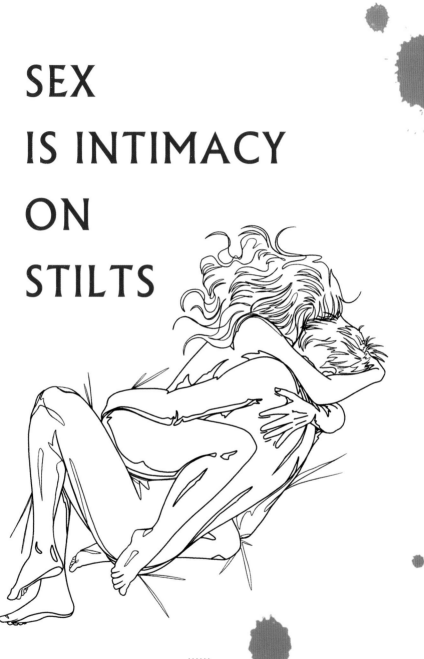

THE MORE
WE LOVE LIFE,
THE MORE WE
FEAR DEATH

FRIENDSHIP IS TO LOVE
WHAT **HOUSE WINE IS**
TO **CHAMPAGNE**

HEARTS,
LIKE THE DAWN,
BREAK SILENTLY

IF MONEY
CAN'T BUY
LOVE,

IT CAN AT
LEAST BUY
LUST

LOVE CAN'T BE BOUGHT, ONLY TRADED-FOR LOVE

ACKNOWLEDGEMENTS

I have dedicated the last two decades of my life to my all-consuming hobby of originating and perfecting my aphorisms. As time went on, I dared to dream that one day I might see them published and enjoyed by readers. For making that dream a reality, I owe my heartfelt gratitude to many people.

Firstly, to my ever-helpful sister Deirdre; to Mohamed Abdelhadi, for his unwavering belief in me and for constantly inspiring me to excel - there's no one else I'd rather spar with; to Charlotte Maddox, who has digested all my 40,000 aphorisms and whom I thank for her dedication and eagle eye for detail.

My thanks also go to Sarah Sadoun for assembling the illustrations and to Huda Hatem for so ably keeping us all on track; to Hamzeh Jundi for his creative input and to Vanessa Duen, Kareem Abdelhadi, Faisal Anani and Orin Willis for their expert technical support. With Eddison Wordplay, I have found the most wonderful team of colleagues and friends.

An extra special thank you goes to designer Aya Talhouni, for her enthusiastic commitment to a book that has brought my aphorisms to life. I am also most grateful to the artists for their evocative illustrations: Kaitlynn Jolley, Elena Richardson, Hadeboga, Kazanina Ekaterina, Elena Golubeva, Darrel Kieene, Leonard Haryanto Purnomo, Sigit Gilal Hartono, Ybchristian

My gratitude also goes to those at Unicorn who helped to guide us on our way.

Finally, I would particularly like to thank Professor Adrian Poole for instituting and running the annual Eddison Aphorism Prize at my old Cambridge college. Inspiring younger generations to find joy and take pride in language is very much what I stand for, and your continued support is invaluable to me.

Thank you to you all, and thank you especially to you, the reader.

First published by Eddison Wordplay Ltd., 2022

22-25 Portman Close
London W1H 6BS
www.ewordplay.com

10 9 8 7 6 5 4 3 2 1

ISBN 978-1-3999-1542-7

Written by Robert Eddison
Designed by Aya Talhouni
Printed by Finetone Ltd.